MOTHERS &
DAUGHTERS

MOTHERS & DAUGHTERS

a photographic celebration

MQP

Don't poets know it
Better than others
God can't be always
   everywhere; and so,
Invented Mothers.

Sir Edward Arnold

Heaven is at the feet of mothers.

Persian proverb

My mother bids me bind my hair
With bands of rosy hue,
Tie up my sleeves with ribbons rare,
And lace my bodice blue.

Anne Hunter

As long as a woman can look ten years younger than her own daughter, she is perfectly satisfied.

Oscar Wilde

I long to put the experience of
fifty years at once into your
young lives, to give you at once
the key of that treasure chamber
every gem of which has cost me
tears, and struggles, and prayers,
but you must work for these
inward treasures yourselves.

Harriet Beecher Stowe

Sweater, n. garment worn by child
when its mother is feeling chilly.

Ambrose Bierce

I wonder how she does it, holding it
together the way she does.

It seems no matter how life gets out of
place she puts it back the way it was.

It's always been a mystery, but I guess it
must be true.

That there is nothing stronger than a
mother's love when she uses Mother's Glue.

Markess A. Wilder

Claudia…remembered that when she'd had her first baby she had realized with astonishment that the perfect couple consisted of a mother and child and not, as she had always supposed, a man and woman.

Alice Thomas Ellis

All women become like their mothers.
That is their tragedy. No man does.
That is his.

Oscar Wilde

My mother is a pretty lady. I wish
to kiss her all day but I have to
go to school.

Tania Price

You never get over bein' a child
long's you have a mother to go to.

Sarah Orne Jewett

"Flowers o' the home"
says he, "Are daughters."

Marceline Desbordes-Valmore

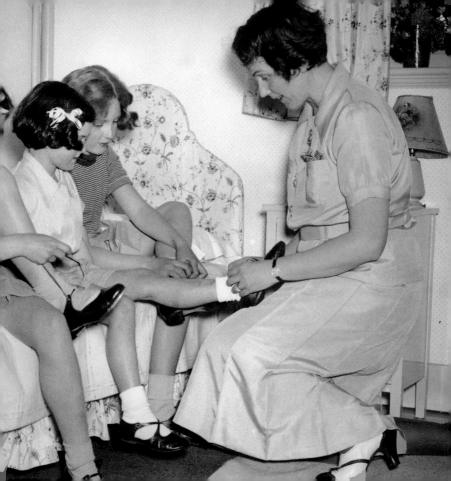

A suburban mother's role is to deliver children obstetrically once, and by car forever after.

Peter de Vries

The moment a child is born, the mother
  is also born.
She never existed before.
The woman existed, but the mother, never.
A mother is something absolutely new.

Rajneesh

How much longer
will I see girlhood
in my daughter?

Eavan Boland

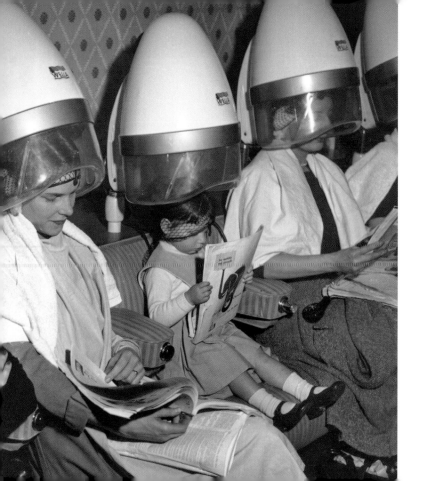

Mrs Morland was a very good woman, and wished to see her children everything they ought to be.

Jane Austen

I am determined to keep my girls walking, walking, walking, but they're determined to keep on talking, talking, talking.

Maria de Selby

A rich child often sits in a poor mother's lap.

Danish proverb

One must leave
one's parents
early, especially
one's mother.
Mothers are never
any good for their
daughters. They
forget they were
just as ugly, and
silly, and scraggy
when they were
little girls.

Mrs Robert Henrey

A mother holds her children's hands
for a while, their hearts forever.

Unknown

One good mother is worth
a hundred schoolmasters.

George Herbert

A mother's love! O holy, boundless thing!
Fountain whose waters never cease to spring!

Marguerite Blessington

My mother had a great
deal of trouble with me,
but I think she enjoyed it.

Mark Twain

My mother wanted
me to be her wings,
to fly as she never
quite had the
courage to do.

Erica Jong

Being a full-time mother is one of the highest salaried jobs in my field, since the payment is pure love.

Mildred B. Vermont

I love you so passionately
that I hide a great part of
my love not to oppress
you with it.

Madame de Sevigne

My mom is a penguin because she is cuddly
My mom is turquoise because she is like the sea
My mom is sunny because she is bright
My mom is an avocado because she is soft
My mom is a pair of boots because she is comfortable
My mom is Top Cat because she makes me laugh.

Molly Line

Oh my son's my son till he gets him a wife,
But my daughter's my daughter all her life.

Dinah Maria Mulock Craik

Mother is one to whom you
hurry when you are troubled.

Emily Dickinson

There's a lass of spirit!
There's my own daughter!

Maria Edgeworth

For some mysterious reason my mother

decided that I would become a more

acceptable person if I learned dancing.

Jennifer Johnston

A fluent tongue is the only thing a mother doesn't like her daughter to resemble her in.

Richard Brinsley Sheridan

O ye loving mothers, know ye
that in God's sight the best of
all ways to worship Him is to
educate the children and train
them in all the perfections of
humankind; and no nobler deed
than this can be imagined.

Bahá'í Sacred Writings

So for the mother's sake the child was dear;
And dearer was the mother for the child.

Samuel Taylor Coleridge

Pick up your litter—
your mother doesn't
work here.

*Sign in a New York
supermarket*

But the child's mother said, "As surely as the Lord lives and as you live, I will not leave you."

The Bible, 2 Kings 4:30

Ha! Here's a roly-poly sprite,
Pa's plaything, and Mamma's delight.

Dinah Maria Mulock Craik

Mama exhorted her children at every opportunity to "jump at de sun." We might not land on the sun, but at least we would get off the ground.

Zora Neale Hurston

79

If you want to understand any woman you must first ask about her mother and listen carefully. Stories about food show a strong connection. Wistful silences demonstrate unfinished business. The more a daughter knows the details of her mother's life— without flinching or whining— the stronger the daughter.

Anita Diamant

Backward, turn backward,
  O Time, in your flight,

Make me a child again
  just for tonight!

Mother, come back from
  the echoless shore,

Take me again to your
  heart as of yore.

Elizabeth Akers Allen

Don't put your daughter on the stage,
Mrs Worthington,
Don't put your daughter on the stage.

Noël Coward

My mum should have been a lawyer—she always managed to persuade me that chores would be fun.

Ethan Hopkins

I believe that always, or almost always, in all childhoods and in all the lives that follow them, the mother represents madness. Our mothers always remain the strangest, craziest people we've ever met.

Marguerite Duras

When thou art feeble, old, and gray,
My healthy arm shall be thy stay,
And I will soothe thy pains away,
My mother.

Jane Taylor

A mother
who is really
a mother is
never free.

*Honoré de
Balzac*

Precepts for the Guidance of a Daughter

Elizabeth Gaskell

Youth fades, love droops, the leaves of friendship fall;
A mother's secret hope outlives them all.

Oliver Wendell Holmes

To her whose heart is
  my heart's quiet home,
To my first love, my
  Mother, on whose knee
I learnt love-lore that is
  not troublesome.

Christina Rossetti

What a beautiful mother,
and yet more beautiful daughter!

Horace

With what price we
pay for the glory
of motherhood.

Isadora Duncan

As is the mother,
so is her daughter.

The Bible, Ezekial 16:44

Motherhood is *not* for the fainthearted. Used frogs, skinned knees, and the insults of teenage girls are not meant for the wimpy.

Danielle Steele

Mother, I love you so
Said the child, I love you more than I know.
She laid her head on her mother's arm,
And the love between them kept them warm.

Stevie Smith

Picture Credits

All pictures © Getty Images, unless otherwise stated.

p.91: A Good Deed, circa 1955.

p.93: A Walk On The Cliffs, circa 1925.

p.95: Teatime, 1939.

p.96: Model Daughters, 1961.

p.99: Chick, 1941.

p.100: On The Beach, circa 1955,
© Lambert/Getty Images.

p.103: Toy Stall, 1949.

p.104: Sewing With Mother, circa 1955,
© Lambert/Getty Images.

p.107: Lockwood And Lockwood, 1953.

p.108: Motherly Love, 1954.

Text Credits

p.4: from *The Future of Motherhood*, by Jessie Bernard. Published by Penguin Books, New York, 1974.

p.16: from "Mother's Glue" by Markess A. Wilder, taken from *In Touch With Every Emotion*.

p.19: from *The Other Side of the Fire*, by Alice Thomas Ellis. Published by Duckworth, 1983. Reprinted by permission of PFD on behalf of Alice Thomas Ellis.

p.23: from *Journeys: Prose by Children of the English-speaking World*, ed. Richard Lewis, Simon & Schuster, 1969. © 1969 by Richard Lewis and used with his permission.

p.33: from "The Blossom" by Eavan Boland, taken from *The Lost Land*, Carcanet Press, 1998.

p.40: from "Paloma" by Mrs Robert Henrey, taken from *Paloma*. Used by kind permission of Madeleine Henrey.

p.50: Extract © Erica Jong.

p.65: from *A Portrait of the Artist as a Young Girl*, ed. John Quinn. Published by Methuen, 1986. © Jennifer Johnston.

p.79: from *Dust Tracks on a Road*, by Zora Neale Hurston. Published by J.B. Lippincott Company, Philadelphia, 1942.

p.80: from *The Red Tent*, by Anita Diamant. Reprinted by permission of St. Martins's Press, LLC. © 1997 by Anita Diamant. Also reprinted by permission of Macmillan, London, UK.

p.84: From "Mrs Worthington" by Noël Coward, taken from *Noël Coward The Complete Lyrics*, ed. Barry Day. Published by Methuen Publishing Ltd, 1998. Reproduced by permission of Methuen Publishing Ltd. © The Estate of Noël Coward.

p.106: Extract © Danielle Steele.

p.109: from "Human Affection" by Stevie Smith. © Estate of Stevie Smith.

Published by MQ Publications Limited
12 The Ivories, 6–8 Northampton Street
London N1 2HY
Tel: +44 (0)20 7359 2244   Fax: +44 (0)20 7359 1616
email: mail@mqpublications.com
website: www.mqpublications.com

Copyright © MQ Publications Limited 2003

Text compilation: Wynn Wheldon
Editor: Laura Kesner

ISBN: 1-84072-571-0

1 2 3 4 5 6 7 8 9

Printed and bound in China